Published in paperback in 2013 by Wayland
Text copyright © Pat Thomas 2013
Illustrations copyright © Lesley Harker 2013

Wayland
Hachette Children's Books
338, Euston Road,
London NW1 3BH

Wayland Australia
Level 17/207 Kent Street
Sydney, NSW 2000

Concept design: Kate Buxton
Series design: Elaine Wilkinson

British Library Cataloguing in Publication Data
Thomas, Pat, 1959-
Why do I feel scared? : a first look at being brave. -- (A
first look at)
1. Fear--Juvenile literature. 2. Courage--Juvenile
literature.
I. Title II. Series
152.4-dc22

ISBN: 978 0 7502 7139 4

Printed in China

Wayland is a division of Hachette Children's Books,
an Hachette UK company.
www.hachette.co.uk

Why do I feel scared?

A FIRST LOOK AT BEING BRAVE

PAT THOMAS
ILLUSTRATED BY LESLEY HARKER

WAYLAND

The world is full of brave people.

But sometimes the
bravest people aren't always
the ones we think they are.

7

Bravery and courage are special gifts.
But they are not something you are born with.

They are choices you make in your heart.

What about you?

Can you think of some brave people you know?

What sorts of things have they done?

There are lots of ways
of being brave.

And not all of them are big and noisy like
in the movies or on TV.

A person becomes brave when they act in a certain way.

Like when they tell the truth, even when other
people don't want to hear it.

Or when they keep trying,
even if they are not very
good at something,
or it is hard...

...or they probably
won't win a prize.

A person is brave when they
are willing to be themselves,
even if it means being a
little different.

And when they stand up for others who find
it hard to stand up for themselves.

Brave people always ask themselves what the right
thing to do is — and then that is what they do.

What about you?

Have you ever done anything brave? Can you think of a time
when you kept trying even when it was hard?

Being brave doesn't mean
you are never afraid.

16

In fact, sometimes if you are afraid there is a good reason.

17

A really brave person would never put themselves, or others, in danger...

...or do something they know is wrong just so others will think they are cool.

And people who are really your friends would never ask you to behave that way.

But sometimes the things we are afraid of seem scary just because they are new, or different, or difficult...

...or because we have never really looked at them properly.

Being brave is a lot like
many things we do every day.

Some days it's easy and some days it's hard.

But you have to practise in order to get good at it.

And the more you practise,
the easier it gets.

The world needs
brave people.

Do you think you could
be one of them?

HOW TO USE THIS BOOK

Courage is an important and powerful, but often difficult to define value. As such it may be best taught 'on the go', through our daily actions and conversations.

When you help your child develop courage you are helping him of her develop the power to say no to things they are uncomfortable with, to not copy their peers' behaviour or 'follow the crowd' when others are behaving in a harmful or destructive way and to protect those who are weaker than they are. But you are also instilling in them the confidence to try new things and to be true to themselves.

Like all aspects of parenting, courage is a lesson best learned in an atmosphere of acceptance and respect. If a child feels safe enough to express his or her fears it will be much easier to explore and eventually outgrow or overcome those fears. As a parent it is important to recognise that all fears – big and small - are real to children. They need to be taken seriously, not punished, or ridiculed or worse ignored.

Some fears are legitimate and age appropriate. Toddlers, for instance, may fear separation from parents, strangers and other unknown things. As a child matures so does his or her imagination and it is not unusual for pre-schoolers and school age children to fear the dark, being left alone, strange animals, being injured or dying and other situations over which they feel they have little control.

A consistent daily routine, where the child knows what to expect, can help with this and can provide children with a sense of power and control.

It is important to recognise your child's moments of personal courage and praise them. It's all too easy, from an adult perspective, to forget how much courage it sometimes takes for kids to do little things. Encouragement and praise from you when your child makes it to the top of the climbing frame, or makes a new friend are very important in helping a child feel safe enough to continue exploring new territory.

Make sure you share your own acts of courage with your children. Don't wait for some big moment of bravery that you can weave into an entertaining tale. Most of us have to do little courageous things every day whether it is meeting the new boss, or speaking up when we see something that is wrong.

Schools can help foster courage by helping children explore the concept in both abstract and practical ways. Using examples from history teachers can introduce the subject of courage. The life stories of others who have faced fear such as Anne Frank or Helen Keller, can be inspirational as well as helping give history a human face. Story time can feature entertaining stories of courage (e.g. *The Wizard of Oz* or *Babe*) and there is a wealth of children's fiction to choose from in this regard.

Group discussions can ask questions like "What is courage?" "Can you think of some examples of courage that you have seen or heard about?", "Does being brave always mean taking risks? Why or why not." Children can be encouraged to talk or write about times they have faced a challenge that required them to be brave, and to express the feeling of that experience and how they overcame their fears.

For parents too, reading to your children is a good way to stimulate thoughts and conversations. There are many children's fiction books that tell tales of courage. What children feel about these stories is often quite revealing. Find ways to weave the themes of those stories in to your daily conversations.

BOOKS TO READ

Babe the Gallant Pig
Dick King Smith (Dell, 1988)

I Feel Frightened
Mike Gordon (Wayland, 2003)

I'll do It: Taking Responsibility
Mike Gordon (Wayland, 1998)

Island of the Blue Dolphins
Scott O'Dell (Yearling Books 1987)

Heroic Stories
Anthony Masters (Kingfisher Books 1994)

Samuel Scaredosaurus (Brian Moses, 2013)

The Children's Book of Virtues
William J Bennett (Simon & Schuster 1996)

The Wonderful Wizard of Oz
Frank Baum (Oxford Children's Classics, 2008)

RESOURCES FOR ADULTS

The Values Book: Teaching Sixteen Basic Values to Young Children
Pam Schiller, Tamera Bryant (Gryphon House, 1998)

Teaching Your Children Values
Lind and Richard Eyre (Fireside, 1993)

The Book of Virtues: a Treasury of great moral stories
William J Bennett (Simon & Schuster 1993)

What Do You Stand For?
Barbara A Lewis (Free Spirit, 1998)